I0837700

BENT THEORY OF ATOMS, ENERGIES AND GRAVITY

A new model for gravity and energies in atoms

Bent Rolf Pettersen

ISBN: 9798658840147

CONTENTS

In all years we have tried to explain gravity with different approaches, from Isac Newton to Albert Einstein. These theories build on assumption on gravity without exact explanation on the phenomenon gravity.

It will be very useful to have an accurate description of gravity for physicists and other scientific personnel.

I have created models of gravity and energy in atom that I believe will provide a comprehensive explanation of gravity, energies and connections in atoms, matter and the universe.

HISTORICAL EXPLANATION – GRAVITY AND ELECTRONS

Gravity, atoms and electricity have been described throughout our history. We will now take a closer look at the historical explanations behind them.

From ancient times and through to the 21st century, people have made numerous attempts to explain gravitational force or gravity.

In ancient times, gravity was seen as a natural part of life, often explained by the presence of the gods. It was perceived as a natural part of existence under the cosmology of the gods, and was explained by the will of supernatural beings.

During the Renaissance (1400–1700), there were many attempts to explain gravity. The earliest among these stemmed from various thinkers who provided the basis for the modern interpretation of gravity.

Examples are early philosophers and astronomers who discerned that the Earth was the centre of the solar system, and that planets orbit the sun. Moons were found to orbit planets. These were kept in place by an invisible force that was called gravitational force.

Planets and moons moved in elliptical orbits, for which several explanations were given. In 1609, Johannes Kepler published a book explaining the planets' elliptical orbits around the sun.

Figure 1: Johannes Kepler (1571–1630)

Figure 2: Galileo Galilei (1564–1642)

In 1632, Galileo Galilei used the terms 'inertia' and 'acceleration' to further explain gravity.

When Isaac Newton formulated his theories in his book 'Philosophiae naturalis principia mathematica' published in 1687, he also formulated 'Newton's law of universal gravitation'.

It explained gravity using the formula:

$$F = G\frac{m_1 m_2}{r^2}$$

where F is the gravitational force acting between objects, G is the gravitational constant, m_1 and m_2 is the mass of the objects, and r is the distance between the objects. needed to move an object,

The law received a mixed response in the strict Christian and patriarchal Europe of the era, but gradually became the leading theory on gravity.

Isaac Newton's theories remained the accepted explanation of gravity for many centuries through to the 20th century, when a number of new theories emerged. The most significant of these were Albert Einstein's theories on gravity, time and light.

Figure 3: Isaac Newton (1642-1727)

Albert Einstein's theories, particularly the general and special theory of relativity, provided a new understanding of gravity and the universe. He also gave us:

$$E = M \times C^2$$

where E is energy, M is mass and C is the speed of light.

Albert Einstein's life work was attempting to explain gravity and connections in the universe. His theories still apply in most fields and are particularly well articulated.

Figure 4: Albert Einstein (1879–1955)

In more recent times, new theories have emerged in the field of quantum theory. Although these theories vary somewhat, they also provide an explanatory model of atomic structure and forces.

Atoms are the building blocks of basic matter and form the basis of our knowledge about elements and the periodic system. The word atom comes from the Greek work atomos, meaning indivisible.

Atomic structure is knowledge that dates back more than 200 years, and is fairly similar today to what it was 100 years ago. New theories have been developed on the structure of atomic nuclei and quarks as well as their effects. There are also new theories about the universe and energies. However, the traditional explanatory models are still prevalent.

I request that you set aside these models when you read and attempt to understand the 'Bent theory of atoms, energy and gravity'.

PREFACE

Atomic bonds give an indication of other bonds in the universe. If you can understand the bonds in an atom, you can understand the universe.

Try to understand the universe and different dimensions and you will understand everything. The universe is vastly complex, in the same way as an atom.

Understand the atom and you will understand the universe.

(Bent Rolf Pettersen ®2019)

We have previously learned that atoms comprise an atomic nucleus made up of neutrons, protons and quantum particles. Electrons spin around the nucleus. Energy is transferred from electrons orbiting the nucleus.

Gravitational force and gravity have seen a wealth of explanations, from Isaac Newton and Albert Einstein's theory of relativity to other more sophisticated explanatory models.

Our fundamental understanding of physics, chemistry and the composition of the universe has spawned from these models.

The interpretations have created challenges in terms of our understanding of atomic structure, energy transfer and the structure of the universe.

This book describes the 'Bent theory of atoms, energies and gravity', which is a new explanatory model in this field.

TERMINOLOGY

A number of new terms are used in the book:

- Ilefos – a force that is applied between matter, gravity, which binds matter together via ilefos tracks.
- Ilefos tracks – a force exerted by matter and stars, which can create bonds between matter (atoms), and stars.
- Free ilefos – ilefos energy that is not bound to ilefos tracks.
- Dielectricity – a main form of energy in atoms and stars.
- Dielectric tracks – dielectric energy emitted from protons in tracks that are attached to ilefos tracks.
- Free dielectricity – dielectricity that is not bound to dielectric tracks.
- Energy – a term used for a number of energies that are not necessarily bound to matter. Pure energy that is not bound to particles or matter that has an extremely high velocity.
- Matter – large systematic accumulations of quarks. These normally comprise neutrons, protons and uniparticles.
- Atomic nucleus – comprises a system of quarks in neutrons and protons.
- Resa – small systematic accumulations of quarks without ilefos and dielectricity tracks.
- Uniparticles – particles that orbit the atomic nucleus and keep the ilefos tracks in place. Uniparticles also ensure distance between the nuclei of different atoms.
- Atomic Phase Displacement – an energy conversion in an atom; the energies that are in the atom and that radiate to and from it.
- Quarks – elementary particles that form atomic nuclei and have specific tasks.
- Plus quark – a quark that is responsible for handling ilefos in atoms.
- Energy quark – a quark that is responsible for handling dielectricity in atoms.

These are key terms in the book and will be described in more detail in dedicated chapters.

THE UNIVERSE

We see the same effects in the universe as we see in atoms. Physics is universal. The same laws of physics apply to the whole universe. All universal phenomena can be explained by the universal physics described in this book, 'Bent theory of energies, gravity and atoms.'

The next book will provide more detail about these theories, and delve deeper into universal phenomena.

It will also include mathematical equations and revised versions of well-known scientific formulas. The book will provide answers to many questions, both known and unknown.

This clears the way for new understanding of physics and the possibilities it entails. It can change our view of physics and open up for new technologies.

ATOMIC STRUCTURE

Atoms are composed of three main parts:

The atomic nucleus, gravitational/energy tracks and uniparticle(s). This is new theory, particularly in relation to uniparticles, and will be elaborated in a separate chapter.

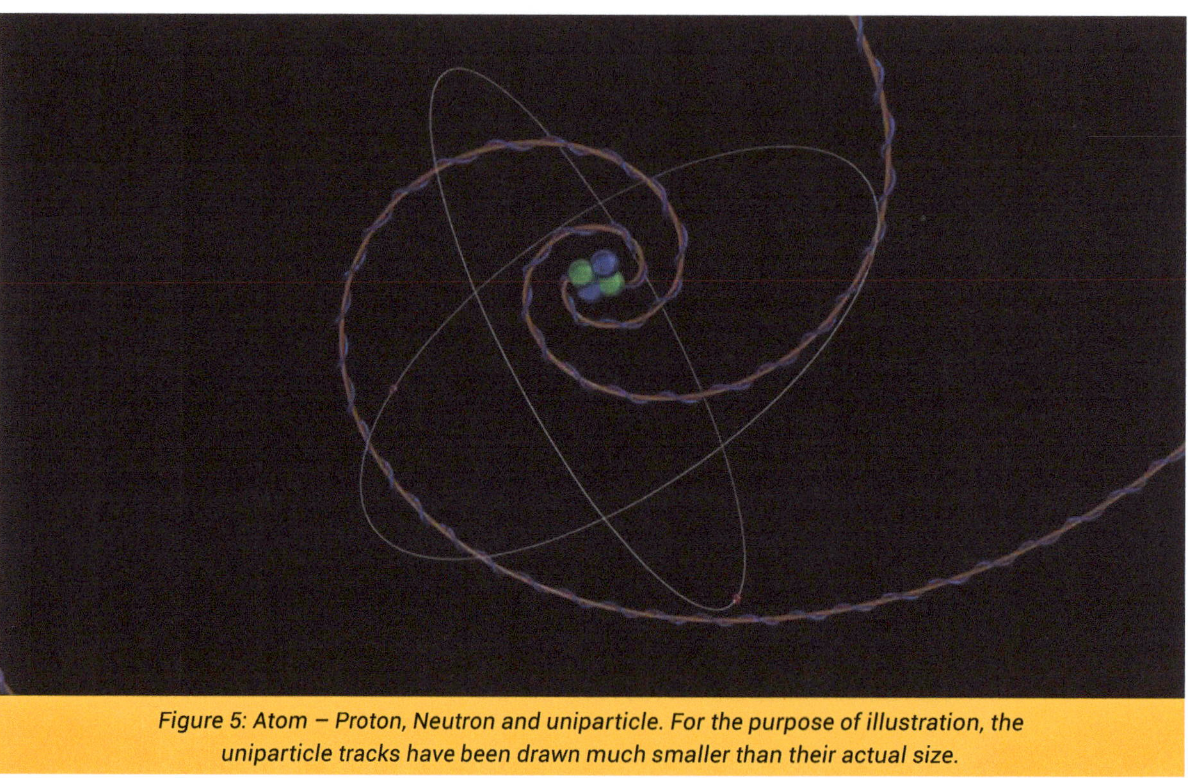

Figure 5: Atom – Proton, Neutron and uniparticle. For the purpose of illustration, the uniparticle tracks have been drawn much smaller than their actual size.

This is fundamental for all matter: normal matter, dark matter and resa.

The atomic nucleus

The atomic nucleus comprises a neutron, proton and quark matter/nuclear matter. Gravitational paths are created in the neutron, and radiate from the neutron in a Fibonacci spiral-like track. This creates a force of attraction/gravity when it comes into contact with the tracks of other atoms. Gravitational paths are called ilefos.

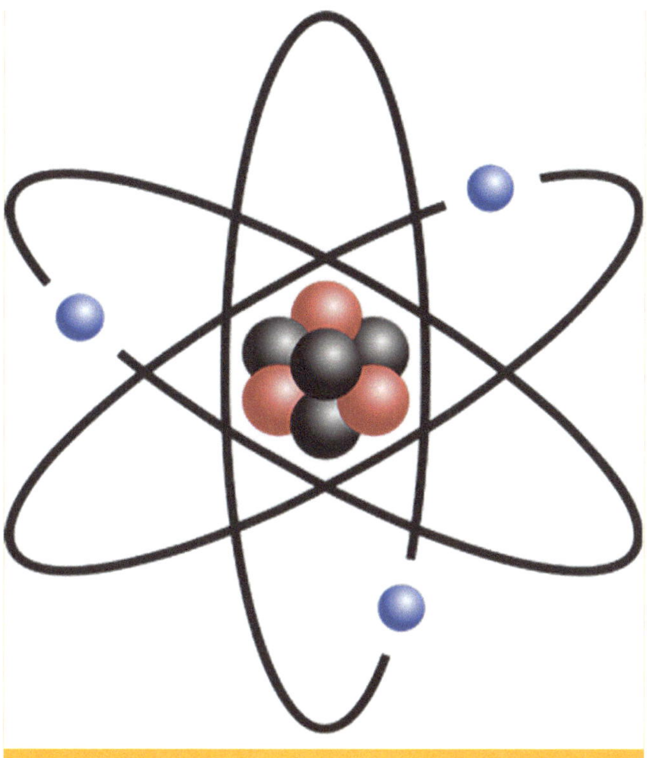

Figure 6: Traditional figure of an atom with proton, neutron and 'electron' (illustration SVG by idolences, Rainer Klute)

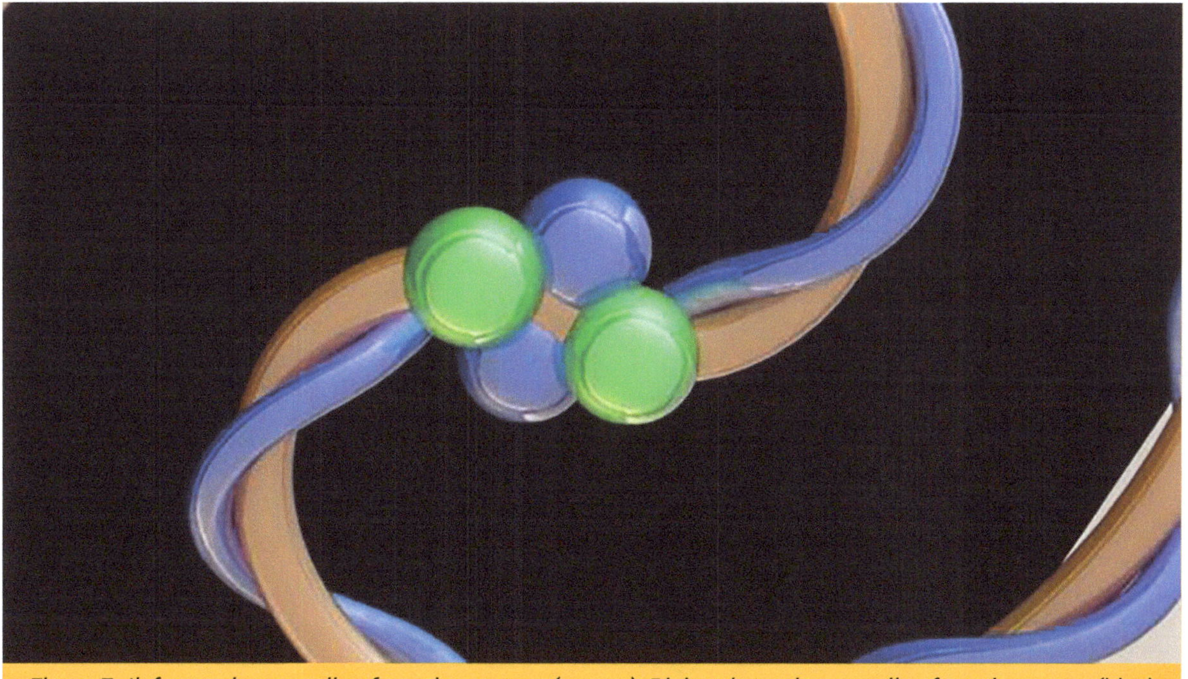

Figure 7- Ilefos tracks extending from the neutron (orange). Dielectric tracks extending from the proton (blue)

Energy tracks are created by the proton. This energy is called dielectricity, often abbreviated to Di. Gravitational paths, or ilefos, have a weak influence on energy tracks, or dielectricity. Dielectricity is bound to ilefos tracks (gravitational paths) when they are created. They are marked in blue in the figure above.

Quark matter is primarily composed of four different types of quark, each with its own special function, which keeps the atom functioning. In all, there are 256 quarks in normal matter. This is further described in the chapter on quarks.

Atoms have their own operating system that runs all processes, quarks, energies and ilefos. These processes are dynamic and immensely advanced and fast. More information is provided about this in the chapter 'Atomic Phase Displacement'.

We will take a closer look at atoms and quark matter later on.

Gravitational paths – ilefos.

Ilefos tracks/gravitational paths are generally created in plus quarks, but can also stem from WE, TE and Tre quarks through Atomic Phase Displacement. Plus quarks transform dielectricity and other energies into ilefos. Ilefos is channelled to the neutron, which processes it and emits it as ilefos tracks in Fibonacci-like pathways.

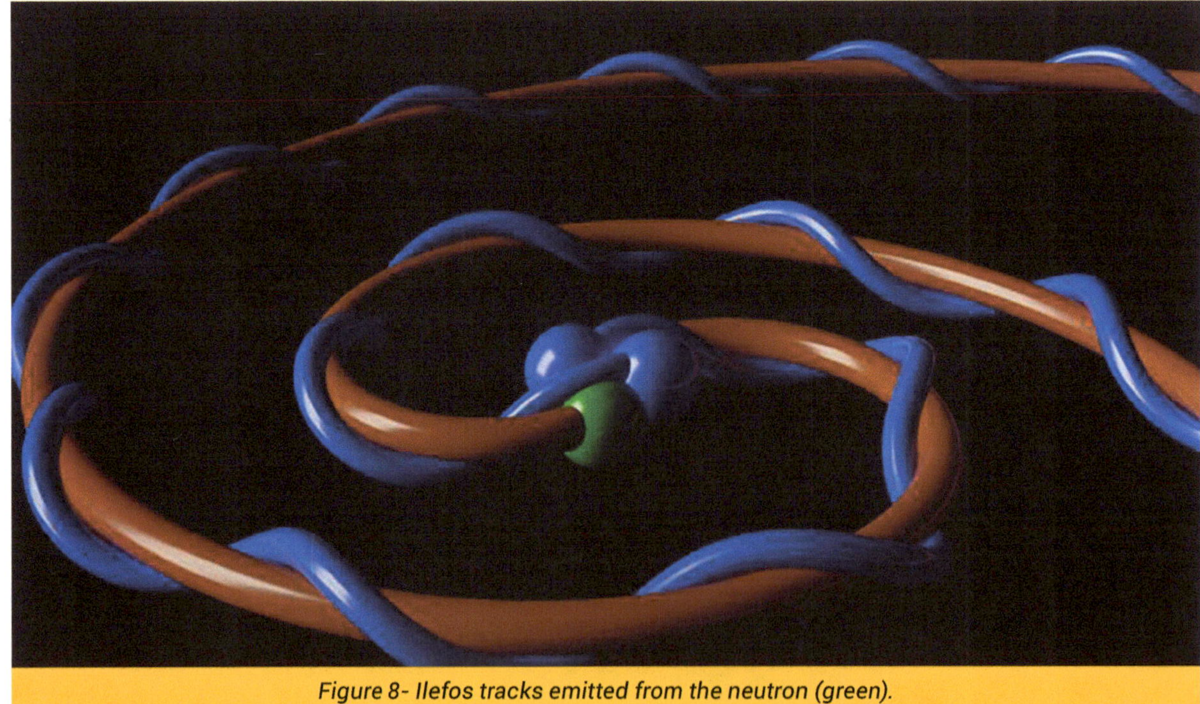

Figure 8- Ilefos tracks emitted from the neutron (green).

These ilefos tracks are attracted by the ilefos tracks of other atoms. The tracks are joined together at intersections. Ilefos tracks can be bound to other ilefos tracks and form a network of bonds to other atoms. The more and stronger bonds, the stronger the gravity or force of attraction. This is further described in the chapter 'Atomic bonds'.

This network also holds atoms together and creates bonds between them, such as molecules and more advanced bonds and structures.

As a rule, gravitational paths are constant, but the track angle can change and affect the number of bonds formed with other ilefos tracks, thereby changing gravity. The track angle and properties of ilefos are called gravitang.

See the chapter 'Gravitang' for a more detailed description.

The ilefos force in tracks can also vary depending on access to energy and the quark composition of the atom. The quark composition and number of neutrons/protons decide the kind of atom we are dealing with.

Ilefos mainly comes from:

- Atoms
- Stars
- Black holes
- Resa
- Gravitational bubbles

This will be further elaborated in the second book, 'Bent theory of Energies, Gravity, Atoms and the Universe'.

Dielectric tracks

Energy tracks or dielectric tracks are normally created in energy quarks.

Energy quarks gather dielectricity from free dielectricity background radiation/free energy radiation and from energy tracks bound together.

Energy is channelled to the proton, which processes it and emits dielectricity in energy tracks/dielectric tracks. Dielectricity may be received and sent out by protons and, and dielectricity attaches itself to ilefos tracks. When attached to ilefos tracks, the dielectric tracks twist around the ilefos tracks in an anticlockwise movement. Dielectricity is therefore weakly attracted to ilefos.

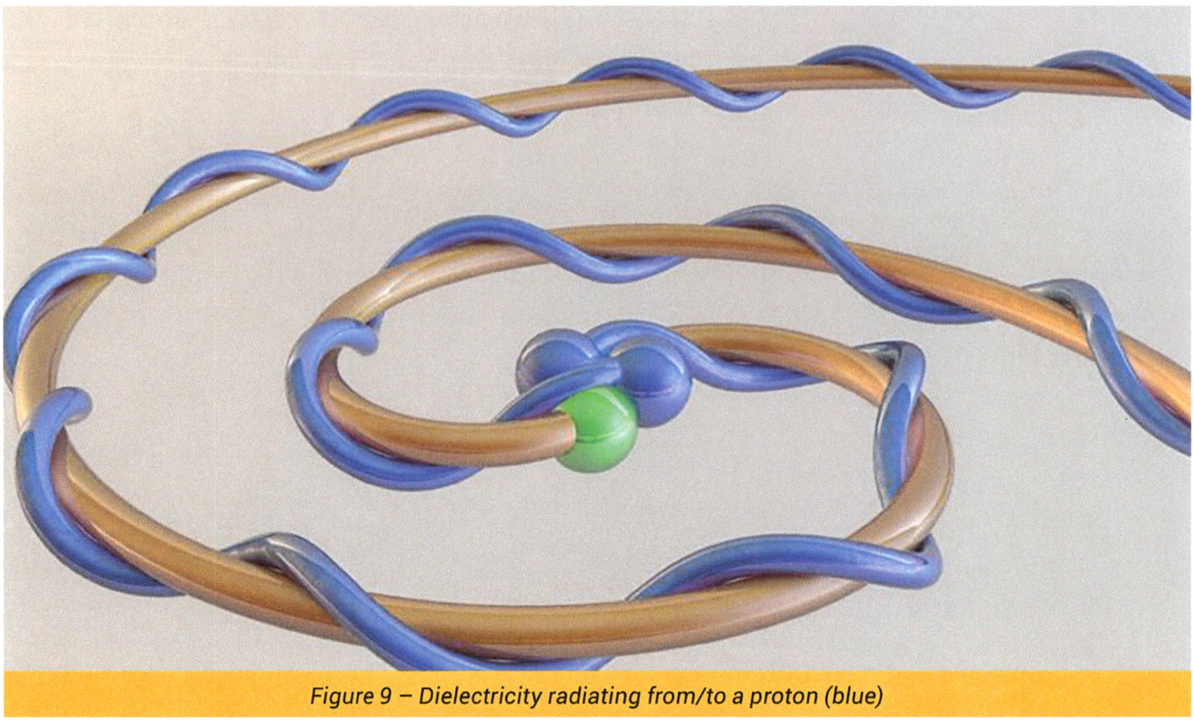

Figure 9 – Dielectricity radiating from/to a proton (blue)

In its free form, i.e. when dielectricity is not bound to ilefos, ilefos is not affected by gravity. Pure dielectricity therefore has an immense velocity of over 7.6 x the speed of light, or over 8,200,000,000 km/h (2,278,422,000 m/s). Free dielectricity that is not bound to the gravitational paths of atoms (ilefos), is the main component of dark energy. This is further described in the chapter 'Dark energy'.

When an atom's ilefos tracks attach themselves to those of other atoms, dielectricity follows the new ilefos track.

The energy level of dielectricity can vary immensely. It is affected by available free dielectricity, dielectricity in the energy tracks bound to it and temperature. A low temperature leads to a low level of dielectricity in the tracks, while a high temperature gives high dielectricity in tracks.

The proportion of dielectricity in tracks can bend and affect the angle of ilefos tracks. This is called Gravitang and will be elaborated in a separate chapter.

Energy transfer between atoms generally takes place via dielectric tracks. Atoms that have strong bonds in the ilefos tracks and extra energy quarks transfer energy well.

Copper, Cu29, has 29 ilefos tracks extending from the atomic nucleus. These are organised such that a large proportion of the ilefos tracks come into contact with the ilefos tracks of neighbouring atoms. On average, 26 of the 29 ilefos tracks from the nucleus will cross the ilefos tracks of neighbouring atoms and form a bond with them (23–27). This makes energy transfer from atom to atom particularly efficient. Copper also has extra energy quarks.

Copper is a conductor, which means that 23–27 energy tracks are in direct contact with other copper atoms via energy tracks, and 2-6 tracks spins, meaning that the tracks do not have contact with other atoms. Copper also has extra energy quarks.

Calcium, Ca20, has 20 ilefos tracks, but only one energy quark. The angles, or gravitang, of these ilefos tracks mean that only a few of the ilefos tracks in the atom meet and bond with those of neighbouring atoms. On average, only 9 of the ilefos tracks meet those of neighbouring atoms. This, along with the fact that calcium only has one energy quark, means that this element has poor energy transfer properties.

This is further described in the chapter 'Atomic bonds'.

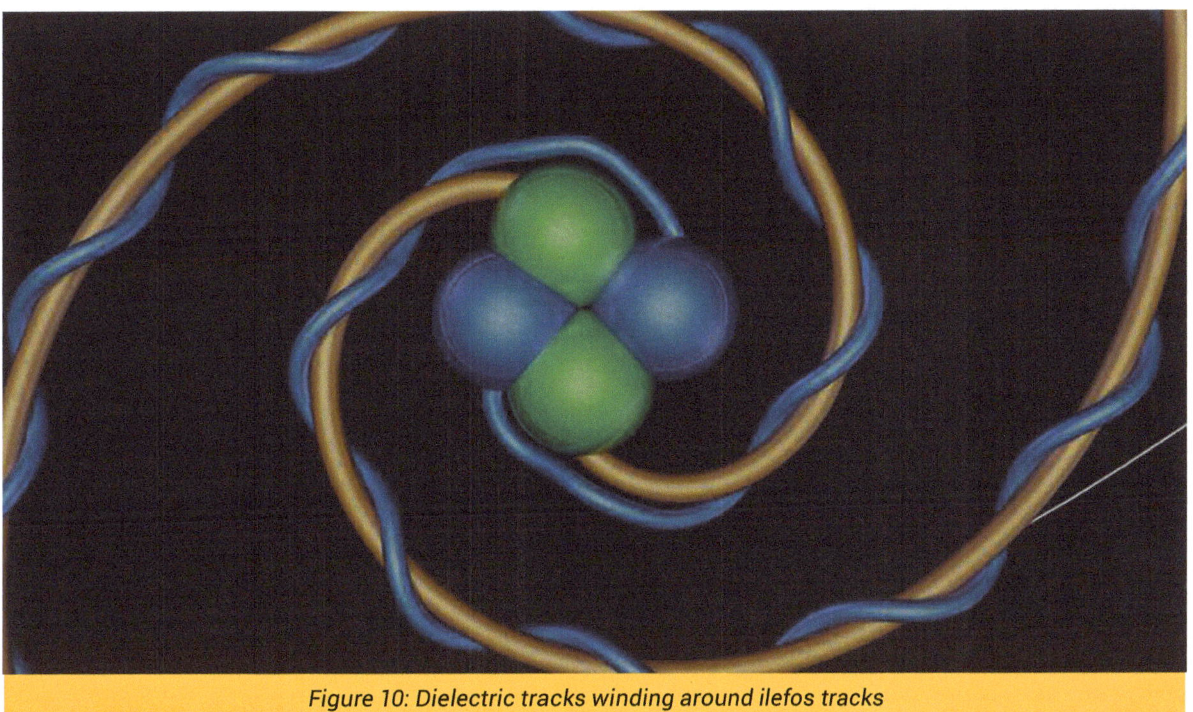

Figure 10: Dielectric tracks winding around ilefos tracks

Uniparticles

A uniparticle is an essential particle that stabilises the atomic nucleus and ilefos tracks.

In principle, the number of uniparticles is equal to the number of neutrons in an atom. Uniparticles have weak gravity and spin around the nucleus creating a gyroscopic effect, which holds the atomic nucleus together and stabilises the ilefos tracks. Uniparticles are smaller in size than neutrons.

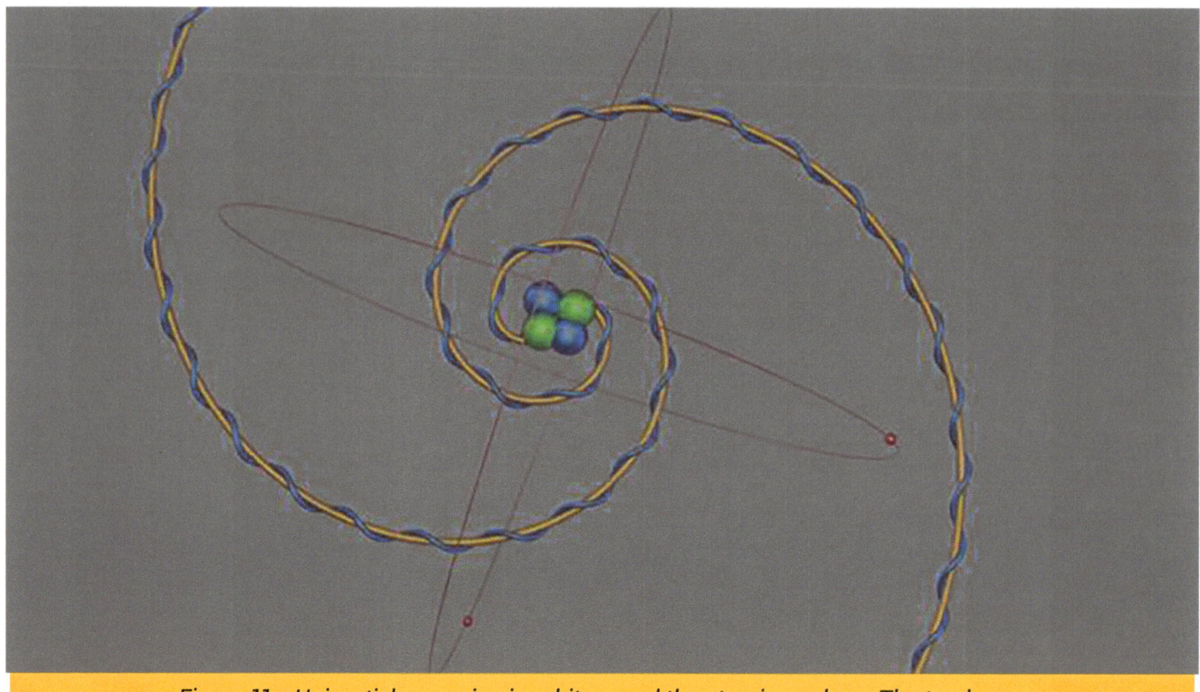

Figure 11 - Uniparticles moving in orbit around the atomic nucleus. The tracks are in fact much wider, but have been reduced for illustrative purposes.

Uniparticles also play an important role in coordinating and transferring signals into and out of the atom. Atoms never come into contact with the uniparticles of other atoms – they keep their distance from one another. Uniparticles have a repulsive force towards other uniparticles. This keeps the atomic nuclei away from each other.

A uniparticle has 5–15 quarks in matter, with an overweight of Tre and energy quarks.

If the uniparticles were to collide or come into contact with one another, it would create an unstable atom. The atom would start to dissolve and explosively emit atomic matter, energies (dielectricity and others) and ilefos. This would cause an uncontrollable chain reaction comprising atomic dissolution and an immensely powerful release of ilefos (gravity) and energy.

A black hole cannot be controlled. It sucks in matter and energy.

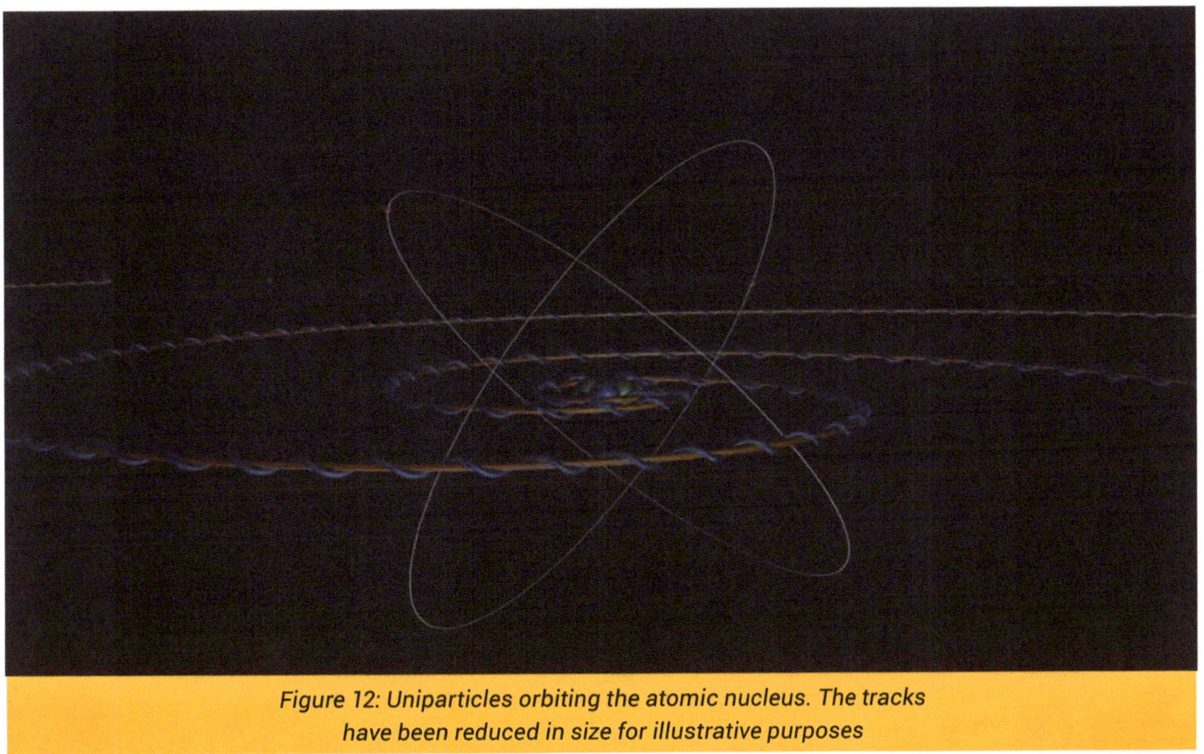

Figure 12: Uniparticles orbiting the atomic nucleus. The tracks have been reduced in size for illustrative purposes

A uniparticle is an essential particle for matter. Without it, matter cannot exist.

ATOMIC BONDS

When bonds are formed between ilefos tracks, atomic bonds are formed. The greater the number of ilefos tracks bound together, the more powerful the atomic bond.

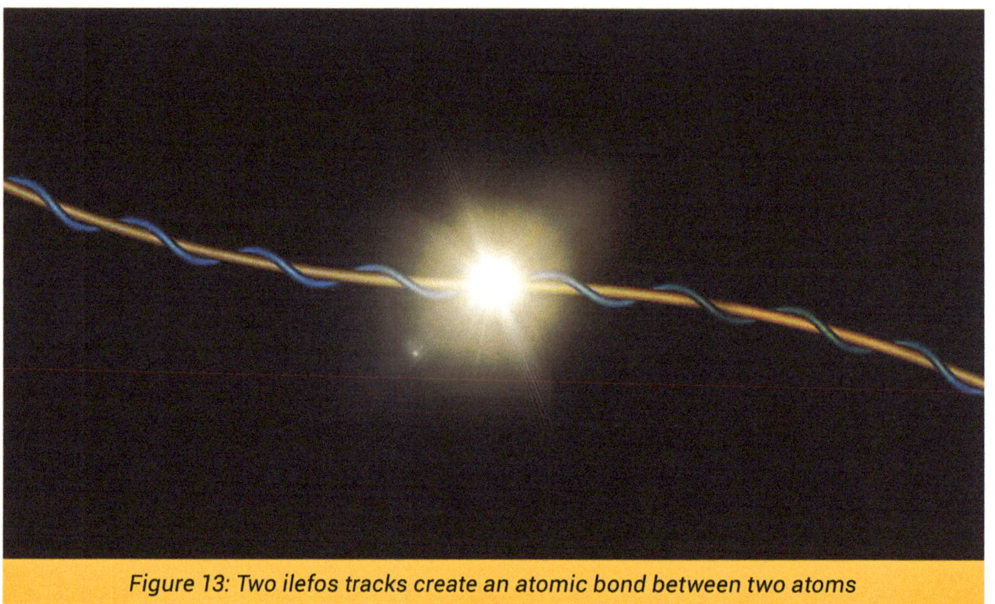

Figure 13: Two ilefos tracks create an atomic bond between two atoms

Atomic bonds are also affected by the strength of ilefos tracks. Powerful ilefos tracks create more powerful atomic bonds. The force of ilefos tracks is decided primarily by the number of plus quarks in a neutron. This, along with Atomic Phase Displacement, creates ilefos tracks. See the chapter 'Atomic Phase Displacement'.

Atomic bonds allow energy to be transferred between atoms via dielectricity tracks. In addition, dielectric tracks absorb free dielectricity and dark energy.

The more powerful and the greater the number of ilefos tracks that are bonded, the more powerful the atomic bonds. The fewer and weaker the ilefos tracks that are bonded, the weaker the atomic bonds.

These bonds hold the atoms together and create molecules and elements. Atomic bonds are a core function of matter and an important function in the universe.

QUARKS

Basic Nuclear quarks:

Nuclear quark type 1:

Basic Nuclear quark type 1:
1. Energy quark
2. Plus quark
3. Negative quark
4. Omega quark
5. ER quark

Basic Nuclear quarks type 2:
6. TE quark
7. Tre quark
8. IS quark
9. IQ quark
10. Plus quark 2
11. Neutral quark
12. Tinga quark
13. Alpha quark (α quark)
14. Omega 2 quark
15. In quark
16. Out quark
17. Positive 3 quark
18. Yr 2 quark
19. Yr 1 quark
20. Yt 1 quark
21. Yt 2 quark
22. TE quark 2
23. Plus quark 3

Quarks are matter found in the atomic nucleus. They have different properties and are put together in a carefully structured system to ensure all of an atom's functions. These are to control energies, ilefos, gravitang, central control and communication processing.

There are 23 basic nuclear quarks. There are also many special quarks. In all, there are 256 quarks in normal matter.

The number of these quarks in an atomic nucleus can vary. A nucleus does not need all 256 quarks but all atoms must have all of the basic nuclear quarks in order to function. All of the basic nuclear quarks exist in all matter.

The number of basic nuclear quarks and special quarks in an atom can vary. The composition of quarks gives an atom its unique properties. The same elements can also have different compositions of quarks. This means that one and the same matter can have different properties. These are called isotopes.

This makes it necessary to extend the periodic system to contain the quark properties of atoms and elements. An element can have several different types of atoms depending on the quark composition. The proposed extension to the periodic system can be found in the second book.

This totals 23 basic nuclear quarks.

Basic Nuclear quark type 1 are quarks that are essential to function. These can often vary in number. The number of plus and energy quarks in particular can vary.

Basic Nuclear quark type 2 are quarks that are normally present in atoms. These are not as essential as type 1 quarks and are generally in the amount 1 quark per proton/ neutron.

Special quarks make up the remaining quarks along with atomic quarks. Special quarks comprise a diversity of quarks that have special properties. They can vary a great deal in type and number and can have many different properties.

Energy-nuclear quarks are located in dense clusters inside the proton. These are placed in a circular grid in which all quarks are in contact with one another. These are called quark Oler.

The other energy quarks are located in the neutron in a similar pattern, quark Oler 2. A very few quarks can be present in both places. These are uni-quarks, which means that they can exist in both places.

Communication between quarks is very fast, including between Olers. It is controlled via control quarks, forming a kind of operating system in the atom. Control quarks are located in the proton and neutron and are called atomic quarks. Atomic quarks are found in addition to basic nuclear quarks and must be present in order for an atom to exist. Atomic quarks are uni-quarks, meaning that they are found in both the proton and neutron.

Communication in the atom takes place during Atomic Phase Displacement. This will be further discussed later on.

Gravity, or ilefos, is controlled by atomic quarks via plus quarks, in addition to a number of smaller quarks.

This is an intricate system that produces, as well as converts and stores, energies and ilefos. The conversion is called Atomic Phase Displacement.

The atomic nucleus thereby comprises:

1. Basic nuclear quark type 1:
2. Basic nuclear quark type 2:
3. Special quarks
4. Atomic quarks

TYPES OF MATTER

In principle, there are two types of matter:

Matter and **Dark matter**. **Anti-matter** and **Resa** are also found, as well as a number of special and rare types of matter.

What distinguishes different types of matter is their quark composition, matter properties and energy level.

Matter

Matter is the dominant atomic form in earth. Normal matter is characterised by a reduced amount of ilefos and dielectric forces in tracks. A normal atom has 256 quarks and 'normal' energy levels. The conversion of energies and gravity takes place in the atomic nucleus, and is moderate via Atomic Phase Displacement. This is due to the atom's quark composition. The composition can vary somewhat and gives the atom its distinct properties.

Figure 14: Normal matter

Matter is the cornerstone of our existence and vital for the existence of living cells. Without matter, we would not have living cells and physical forms as we know them.

About 4.5% of the universe is made up of normal matter. Dark matter makes up around 25.5% and resa about 1.5% . Resa is a new variant of matter, and is

Figure 14: Normal matter

described in more detail in a separate chapter. Normal matter thus makes up about one sixth of all matter in the universe.

Matter makes up 31.5% of the universe. Dark energy makes up 68.5% of the universe. This is known information.

Matter forms the basis of our existence and the elements found in the periodic system.

The composition on Earth is about 35% matter, 15% dark matter and 50% dark energy.

Dark matter

Dark matter is the dominant matter in the universe. It makes up around 25.5% of the universe.

Dark matter is characterised by having different properties to normal matter. Dark matter has much more powerful ilefos and energy than normal matter. This is because its quark composition is different to that of normal matter.

On average, normal matter has 256 quarks in the nucleus, i.e. neutrons and protons.

Dark matter has much more powerful ilefos and energy tracks than normal matter. It also has more powerful uniparticles. This is because dark matter has more quarks than normal matter. In general, the nuclei of dark matter contain 298 quarks compared to 256 in normal matter.

Dark matter has new quarks, which normal matter does not. These include uni-quark 2, which reinforces the uniparticles holding particles/the nucleus together. Dark matter has energy quarks 3 and 4, which enable greater energy storage in the nucleus. It also has plus quark 2, which allows more powerful ilefos tracks.

Energy, ilefos and uniparticles are controlled via Atomic Phase Displacement. This is an automatic 'operative system' that is run locally in the nucleus.

On Earth, dark matter is mainly found near the Earth's core due to strong ilefos bonds. Dark matter is also found in 'looser bonds' on the Earth's surface, but only in tiny amounts.

Dark matter contains more than 256 quarks. It has everything from 291 to 320 quarks, with the normal number being 298. The quark composition is dependent on how much energy it has received.

Matter in the universe that is exposed to strong energy or ilefos – more than Atomic Phase Displacement can manage to handle – automatically makes more quarks to handle the large amounts of energy. Normal matter then becomes dark matter. Dark matter can make and handle larger amounts of energy and ilefos.

This takes place, among other things, when matter passes through gravitational/ilefos bubbles, or areas containing vast amounts of energy. Ilefos bubbles are described in the chapter 'Gravitational fields'.

Dark matter sucks in energy and quarks from the surroundings where these are easily available. It absorbs all energy and quarks from protons. Photons are not reflected for this reason. Dark matter is therefore 'invisible' in the sense that it does not reflect light and appears to be entirely black.

Figure 16: Dark matter absorbs energy and photons and is therefore entirely matt without any reflections

RESA

There are three types of Resa matter: Resa 0, Resa and Resa +.

Resa 0 is quark matter that has not been put together to form matter, but is held together without ilefos or uniparticles. The weak bonds that hold quark matter together use quarks' built-in gravity. There are 6–50 quarks held loosely together.

Resa is quarks that form bonds with the neutron, but without ilefos. Here, the uniparticles hold the quarks together. Resa has light neutrons, protons and only uniparticles. They are very closely packed together and have minimal gravity.

Resa can be created in places without gravity, but where the other quark matter is present. This often concerns high levels of Tre energy and dielectricity – enough to create nuclear and uniparticles. The uniparticles then hold the nucleus in place. Uniparticles have a high velocity and high energy level. The 'nuclei' are held densely together. Resa is a thousand times more dense than a normal atom and has strong bonds. Bonding takes place through direct attraction between atomic nuclei.

Resa makes up around 1.5% of the universe. It is mainly found between galaxies and stars since it has minimal gravity. Resa emits some energy and a minimal amount of ilefos. Energy is released directly from the proton; ilefos from uniparticles is minimal.

Resa normally has 51–160 quarks in the nucleus, i.e. proton.

Resa is one of the five main types of matter: Resa, matter, anti-matter, dark matter and dark anti-matter.

Resa + is a denser form of resa that has 161–250 quarks. Resa + does not have ilefos or dielectric tracks. It has the same properties as Resa, but is heavier.

OXYGEN

Oxygen is a special atom that has 8 protons and neutrons. It has good contact properties, which means that the atom's ilefos tracks are more powerful and more readily form bonds with other atoms. This is because oxygen has an additional plus quark in its neutrons. It therefore has somewhat more powerful ilefos tracks than other gases. Oxygen has 8 ilefos tracks and 8 uniparticles.

Traditional illustration of oxygen (Greg Robsom):

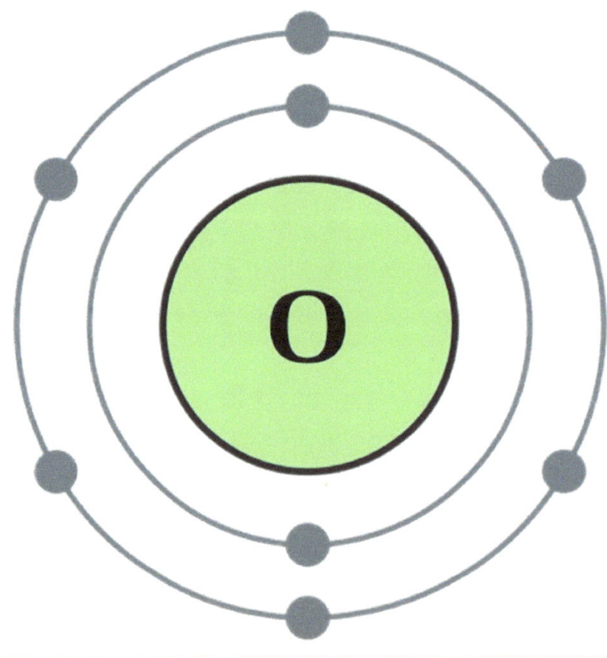

Figure 17: Traditional illustration of an oxygen atom

Figure 18: Oxygen has 8 ilefos tracks and extra energy quarks.

Due to its additional plus quarks, oxygen transfers more gravity/ilefos than normal atoms. This is called gravity 23 (see glossary). Oxygen transfers ilefos more efficiently than other gases. Matter will therefore have more gravity in oxygen. Oxygen has more powerful ilefos than Helium (He), Hydrogen (H) and Nitrogen (N).

Oxygen also has particularly good energy transfer properties, since it also has additional energy quarks. This means that oxygen is more capable of receiving and emitting energy, mainly in terms of dielectricity. This takes place via protons. Protons can emit and receive energy or dielectricity via the atom's dielectric tracks, where dielectric tracks follow the ilefos tracks.

In our bodies, energy from oxygen is transferred to the blood via red blood cells. The red blood cells attach to the oxygen atoms without absorbing the oxygen's energy. The oxygen is then transported to the areas that need oxygen, where oxygen bonds with other atoms and release energy. During this process, oxygen bonds with carbon that is void of energy. This bond, CO_2, attaches to the red blood cells, which transport CO_2 from the body.

Oxygen gives energy to plants through a similar process. This takes place via H_2O (water), which plants absorb through their roots. A process using energy from photons then splits H_2O into hydrocarbons (with CO_2) and oxygen. Plants and algae receive more energy from photons than they can manage to store. The oxygen is filled up with energy and released. This energy is primarily stored in energy quarks, but some is also stored in other quarks. Oxygen also receives some energy from free dark energy.

It is therefore an essential atom for living cells.

The atomic structure of oxygen is as follows:

	Atom: Oxygen	Number of quarks
	Basic nuclear quarks type 1:	
1	Energy quark	3
2	Plus quarks	2
3	Negative quark	1
4	Omega quark	1
5	ER quark	1
	Basic nuclear quarks type 2:	
6	TE quark	1
7	Tre quark	1
8	IS quark	1
9	IQ quark	1
10	Plus quark 2	1
11	Neutral quark	1
12	Tinga quark	1
13	Alpha quark (α quark)	1
14	Omega 2 quark	1
15	In quark	1
16	Out quark	1
17	Positive 3 quark	1
18	Yr 2 quark	1
19	Yr 1 quark	1
20	Yt 1 quark	1
21	Yt 2 quark	1
22	TE quark 2	1
23	Plus quark 3	1
		26

Oxygen has 26 nuclear quarks. These are divided between the protons and neutrons. There are also special quarks bringing the total number of quarks to 259.

ISOTOPES

Isotopes are variants of matter that have special properties. These properties can vary depending on the quark composition. Most commonly, certain types of matter have additional energy quark(s). This gives the matter other properties than are found in the original matter. Isotopes of matter can also lead to the matter having other contact properties. It is in such case the change in the number of negative quarks that leads to extra ilefos properties.

Isotopes can also have other special properties, which we will return to in the second book.

DARK ENERGY

Dark energy makes up 68.5% of the universe. Dark energy is energy that is not attached to matter or quarks. Dielectricity becomes dark energy after dielectricity release, i.e. when it becomes detached from atoms and ilefos. This is further described in the chapter 'Dielectricity release'. The same thing happens to ilefos as a result of ilefos release. This is described in more detail in the chapter 'Ilefos release'.

Dark energy is primarily composed of:

Dielectricity	79%
Ilefos	13%
Tre energy	1.5%
ER energy	1.2%
Yr energy	1.1%
WE energy	1%
Omega energy	3.2%
	100%

Figure 19: The universe seen through a Hubble telescope (ESA)

These energies will be further discussed in the second book.

Dark energy is everywhere in the universe, but can be more powerful in certain places. Dark energy is free energy and remains free until it attaches itself to matter or other atomic bonds, such as stars, black holes, photons or resa.

DIELECTRICITY RELEASE

Dielectricity normally follows the ilefos tracks extending from an atom. Here, the dielectricity winds anticlockwise around the ilefos track. Dielectricity follows the ilefos track until ilefos becomes too weak to hold the dielectricity, at which point the attachment is broken. We refer to this as dielectricity release.

It is caused by the ilefos tracks becoming weaker with distance from the atomic nucleus. In a normal atom at 20°C, and with normal levels of dielectricity and ilefos, dielectricity release takes place in the ilefos track approximately 100 km from the atomic nucleus. At higher temperatures, dielectricity release will take place further away from the nucleus, while at lower temperatures, it will take place further in.

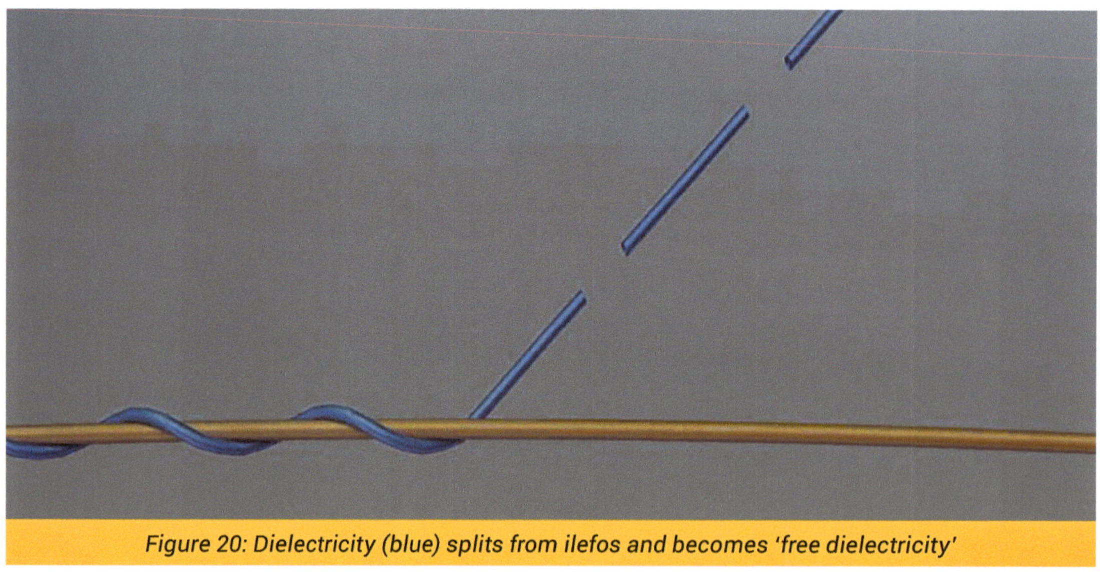
Figure 20: Dielectricity (blue) splits from ilefos and becomes 'free dielectricity'

When dielectricity release occurs, the dielectricity breaks free from ilefos and is split into smaller fragments of dielectricity. We then have free dielectricity, which is a main component of dark energy.

Free dielectricity moves extremely fast since it does not have any connections. It continues on a set path until it is absorbed by matter, quarks, stars or black holes. Free dielectricity has no mass and moves at a speed of 7.6 times the speed of light. This is described in more detail in the second book.

ILEFOS RELEASE

Following the release of dielectricity, the ilefos track continues some distance further. Ilefos tracks become weaker with distance from the atom or source. Ilefos becomes weaker and weaker until it becomes free ilefos, i.e. it is broken down and loses contact with its source. This is when ilefos release occurs.

The further the ilefos tracks are from the atomic nucleus, the more they lose their force of attraction. When an ilefos release takes place, we are left with 'free ilefos'. Ilefos that has been broken down and lost contact with its atom or source goes straight out into the universe where it forms part of dark energy.

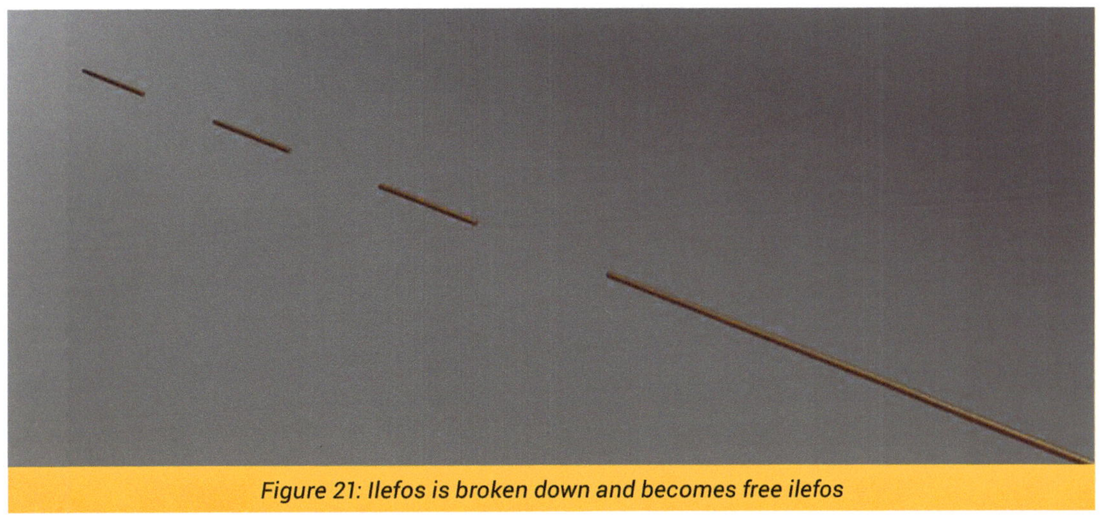

Figure 21: Ilefos is broken down and becomes free ilefos

Free ilefos can become attached to other loose ilefos and form a gravitational field. Free ilefos has gravity, but not as powerful as that of ilefos attached to atoms.

In a normal atom at a temperature of 20°C, ilefos release takes place in the ilefos track at approximately 19,000 km from the nucleus. At higher temperatures, ilefos release takes place further out, and at lower temperatures, it occurs closer to the atomic nucleus. This also depends on the force of the ilefos tracks, which in turn depends on the properties of the atom (number of plus quarks in the matter).

Free ilefos continues on a straight path until it is collected in gravitational bubbles or absorbed by matter, quarks, stars or black holes.

NASA's spacecraft Voyager discovered magnetic fields at the edge of the solar system, which are characterised by 100-km-wide magnetic bubbles. These are gravitational bubbles or gravitational fields. A gravitational field is a mass of ilefos with no attachment to matter or dark matter, i.e. pure ilefos subsequent to ilefos release.

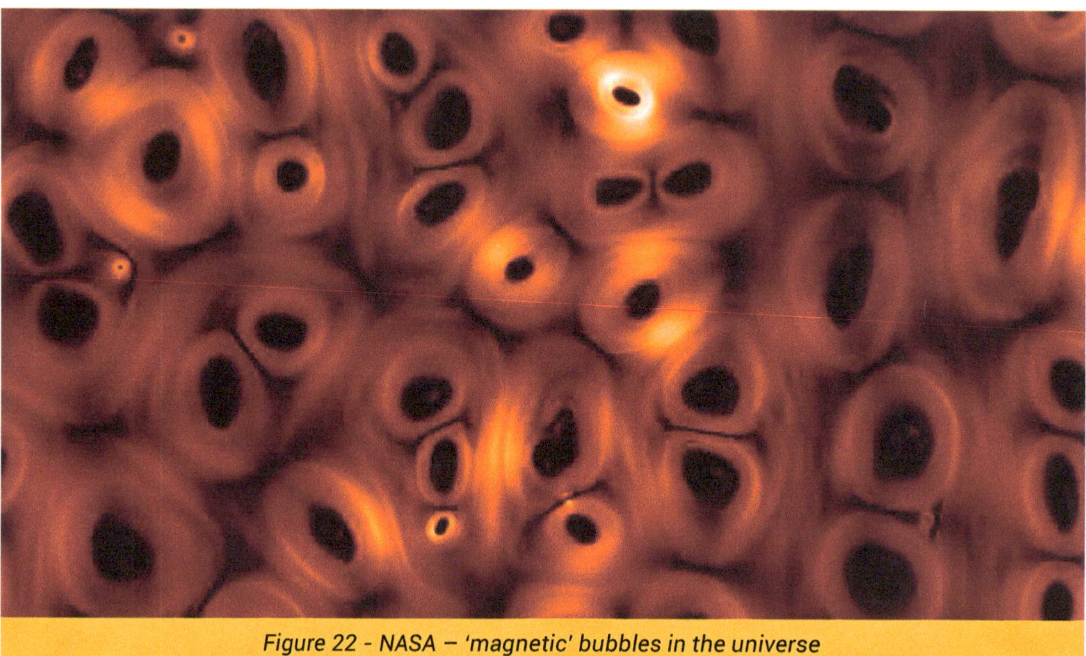

Figure 22 - NASA – 'magnetic' bubbles in the universe

This is a 'mass' of gravity that has a bubble-like form. It has weak gravity and can attract matter and energy.

Gravitational bubbles, which are accumulations of free ilefos clumped together, primarily comprise pure ilefos, with some amount of resa. This affects photons and matter in the universe, which can be observed through a telescope.

In general, the speed and energy with which matter moves is too great for the ilefos bubbles to manage to hold on to the matter. When matter passes a large ilefos bubble, it receives enormous amounts of ilefos, which is stored in quarks; primarily in plus quarks. The huge amount of ilefos added is transformed through Atomic Phase Displacement to other forms of energy that are stored in their representative quarks. If the quarks contained in the matter do not manage to handle this amount of energy, the matter can create more quarks to do so. These are generally plus and energy quarks, but other nuclear quarks can also be created. This is one way in which dark matter is formed.

Matter that has passed through an ilefos bubble will be fully-charged with energies. This charged matter can change its quark composition in order to handle the enormous amounts of energy received when passing through the ilefos bubble, and matter thus becomes dark matter.

Dark matter is very rich in energy and has extremely powerful ilefos and energy tracks.

PHOTONS

Photons are particles charged with dielectricity. These particles have been detached from atoms. They become detached from the atomic nucleus when the nucleus receives too much dielectricity. The nucleus is then unable to hold on to the energy, and energy and particles are released from the nucleus via energy tracks. Particles are extra quarks, which are made by atom to handle the extra energy. These particles have mass and detach from the ilefos tracks almost instantaneously.

Particles are detached quark matter. This matter comes from energy quarks, which are primarily found in protons. Such quark matter is fully-charged with dielectricity. This is also called light. Photons generally move at the speed of light.

Figure 23: Light bulb – an example of a source of photons

When photons are produced, energies and quark matter is released to the surroundings. Among other things, this takes place in the sun when atomic nuclei are split and atoms rid themselves of energy.

The charged photons move quickly and are very little influenced by ilefos/gravity. Photons retain dielectricity until they meet matter, resa, stars or black holes. When this happens, they emit energy (dielectricity) and quark matter.

Figure 24: The sun – our biggest source of photons

Photons, or light, are quark matter that can be emitted from matter or stars. It is then emitted by the atom's protons and attaches itself for an instance to ilefos. This quark matter attracts ilefos, but has its own mass that means it detaches from ilefos tracks just after release.

The composition of quark matter and the energy level determine the type of photon, or the light's wavelength.

Photons' energy stems from quark matter, and it sucks up dark energy as it goes along, like an atom. Photons become more dependent on the surroundings over greater distances. Matter, resa, stars and black holes drain photons of their energy. Dark energy supplies photons with more energy. Photons are living quark matter.

Figure 25: The sun's surface – photo Inouye Solar Telescope NSO/AURA/NSF

An atom has on average 256 quarks, while a photon has 3–5. When detaching from an atom, quarks divide to create quark matter for photons.

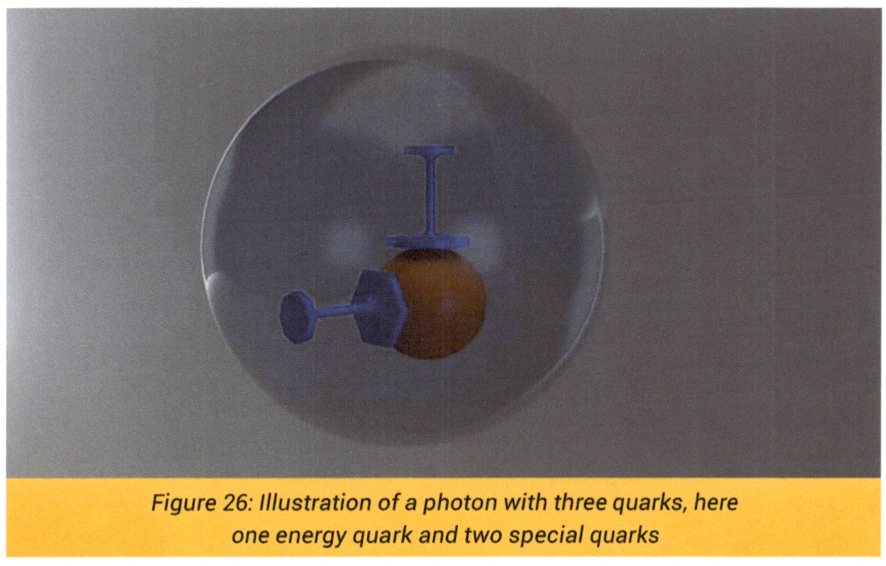
Figure 26: Illustration of a photon with three quarks, here one energy quark and two special quarks

The quark composition of certain types of matter make them suitable for producing photons. This matter then has additional energy quarks. When adding energy to an atom, certain atoms will emit this energy as photons.

ATOMIC PHASE DISPLACEMENT

Atomic Phase Displacement is energy conversion in the atomic nucleus. This is where energy is converted and stored via quarks. The process is immensely fast. Energy also go opposite way out of quarks when this is needed.

In Atomic Phase Displacement, free energy and energy in an atom is converted. In general, atoms receive and emit energy via ilefos tracks. Atomic Phase Displacement converts dielectricity, ilefos, Tre energy, ER energy, Yr energy, omega energy and other energies into the desired form of energy. This is primarily dielectricity and ilefos, which is emitted through ilefos tracks.

Atomic Phase Displacement takes place in all atoms. It occurs in neutrons and protons and determines what is emitted from/ stored in an atom/matter. This is described in more detail in the second book.

Atomic Phase Displacement stores excess energy in quarks. It draws on this energy when necessary or when instructed to.

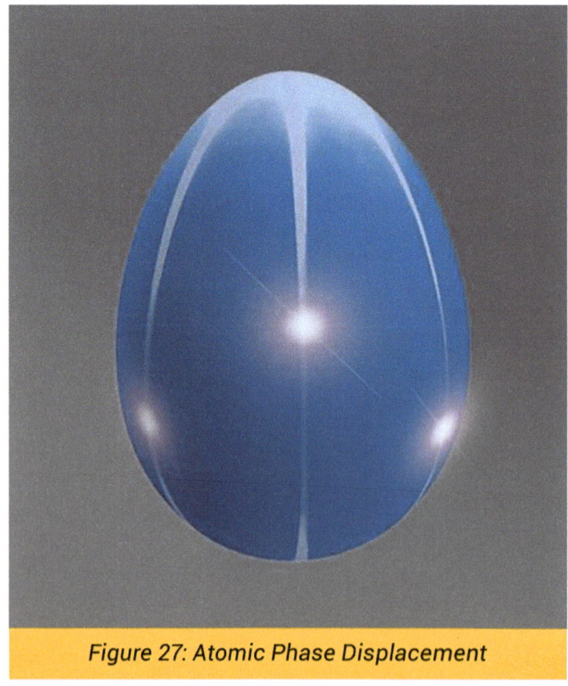

Figure 27: Atomic Phase Displacement

Illustration: proton, with energy centre in the middle – flash of energy when the conversion in the quarks occurs. Energy tracks from the top where energy enters and exits the proton.

MAGNETISM

Magnetism is when ilefos and dielectricity tracks properties of a matter change. This could be both on a permanent basis or as a result of the powerful transfer of dielectricity.

In a permanent magnet, ilefos tracks are changed, making them more powerful and 'straighter'. This makes it easier for them to form bonds with atoms that have similar tracks. Quarks are changed making the ilefos tracks extremely powerful, with a moderate content of dielectricity.

Magnets are strongly attached to iron, since iron has very similar ilefos tracks and a quark composition that makes it absorb ilefos, which is stored as energy in the nucleus via Atomic Phase Displacement.

Iron has extra plus quarks, roughly twice the normal amount, that make it able to store particularly large amounts of ilefos energy.

In a permanent magnet, dielectric tracks are changed enabling the atoms to receive extra dielectricity from dark energy. This extra dielectricity is transformed to ilefos during Atomic Phase Displacement. Atoms emit particularly powerful and straight ilefos tracks for this reason. This constitutes a permanent change in ilefos and dielectric tracks.

Metal/iron then becomes a 'dielectricity antenna', which absorbs dielectricity from dark energy and emits powerful straight ilefos tracks (magnetic matter).

Electro-magnets receive great amounts of dielectricity that moves freely through copper. Copper is saturated with dielectricity and does not absorb more. Copper sends the dielectricity though dielectricity tracks on to iron, which converts it through Atomic Phase Displacement to ilefos, creating powerful and straight ilefos tracks. Copper does not have the capacity to absorb the ilefos emitted from iron or transfers it. Ilefos tracks or magnetic fields from the iron, follows the dielectric direction but on the outside of the copper, where it is then drawn back towards the iron nucleus.

If other 'magnetic' objects such as iron come in close proximity of these tracks, they are drawn towards the ilefos tracks.

GRAVITANG – ILEFOS TRACK ANGLE

Ilefos can have different track angles. The angle of ilefos tracks from the neutron is gravitang, which is a measurement of the force and angle of ilefos tracks.

Gravitang is thus a measurement of how ilefos behaves in different phases. This is because ilefos tracks can behave differently depending on temperature/how much ilefos force the tracks contain.

High energy levels in dielectricity and ilefos tracks increase the angle of the ilefos tracks, while low energy levels decrease the angle.

Figure 28: Three types of gravitang. First low/ normal gravitang with low/ normal ilefos. Second strong gravitang with high angle and and high ilefos power in ilefos tracks. Third very high gravitang and very high ilefos power in ilefos tracks.

The third example in figure above are found in stars and places with high energy/temperature.

Low temperatures lead to a low angle and low energy level of dielectricity in the ilefos tracks. At extremely low temperatures, ilefos tracks have almost no ilefos force and a very low angle.

The ilefos tracks of **superconductors** are extremely weak. This means that the atom has almost no energy available for ilefos and dielectric tracks. The ilefos tracks in such case become so weak that they are drawn back in towards the nucleus. The tracks emitted from the neutron then move inwards again towards the nucleus. The atomic nucleus is still held in place by uniparticles and the atomic nucleus itself. Gravitang then becomes negative.

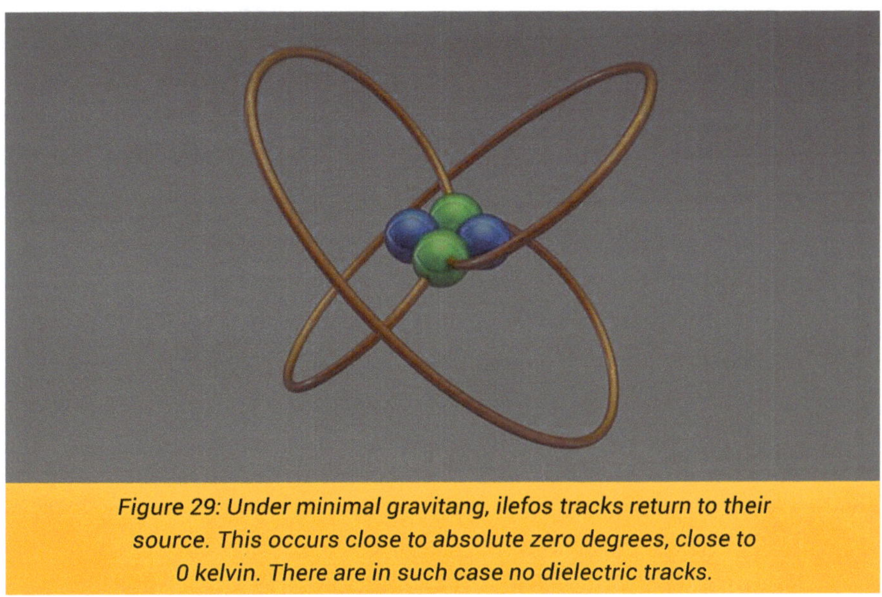

Figure 29: Under minimal gravitang, ilefos tracks return to their source. This occurs close to absolute zero degrees, close to 0 kelvin. There are in such case no dielectric tracks.

Illustration: At -273 °C, -459 °F or 0 °K, there are no dielectric tracks. Ilefos tracks are weak and are drawn back towards the atomic nucleus.

Dielectricity that is added then jumps from track to track, leading to very little resistance as seen in the illustration below. This because the ilefos tracks are too weak to affect the dielectricity track.

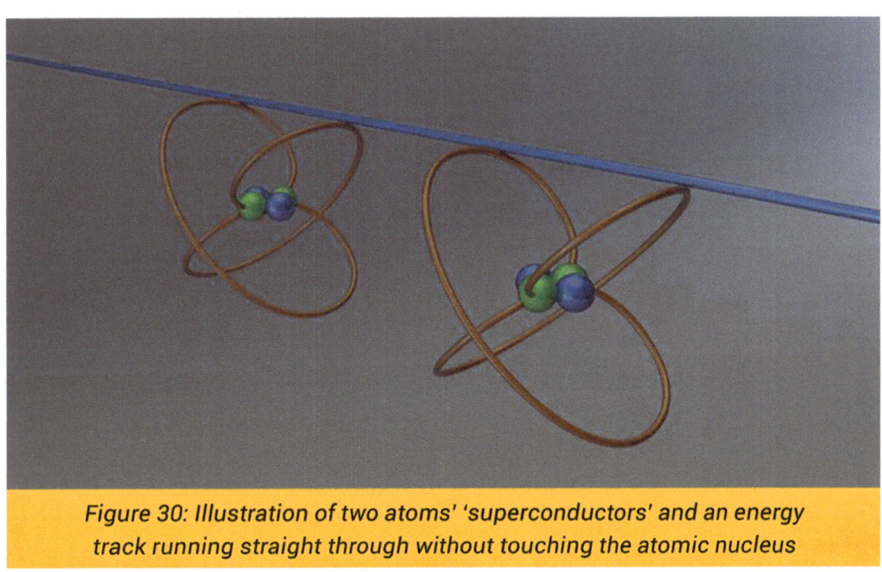

Figure 30: Illustration of two atoms' 'superconductors' and an energy track running straight through without touching the atomic nucleus

Gravitang is documented, described in more detail and shown in mathematical formulas in the next book.

RADIOACTIVE ELEMENTS

Radioactive elements have a distinct quark composition. They have additional Tre, Te and energy quarks.

A neutron and proton have:

Quarks	Radioactive elements	Normal elements
Plus quarks	3 (2-5)	1 (1-3)
Energy quark	3 (2-5)	1 (1-3)
Tre quark	2 (2-3)	1 (1-2)
TE quark	2 (2-3)	1 (1-2)

Normal number, in brackets 'possible number'.

The atom thus has extra energy from energy quarks, Te quarks, ER quarks and Tre quarks. Atoms therefore emit extra energy, primarily dielectricity, but also energy in other forms.

Tre and Te energy run directly from the proton and not via ilefos tracks, since these are not affected by ilefos (gravity). They have the ability to affect cells if their quantities are too great.

Too much Tre and Te energy can lead to other living cells dividing too quickly. Tre energy in particular can overload Tre quarks and send division signals in order to relieve Tre quarks. This is a recurring experience transfer that entails changes to the cell's DNA. This is known as cancer. This process is described in more detail in the second book.

The next book will take a closer look at the concepts introduced here and provide more detailed explanations. It will also delve deeper into the universe and universal phenomena and connections, and touch on spacetime (omega). The next book will also introduce a new method for systematising matter in relation to the number of nuclear quarks it contains.

Bent Rolf Pettersen — 2019 ©

GLOSSARY

Anti-matter
- Matter that does not have uniparticles. Very unstable matter.

Atomic bonds
- Bonds between atoms where the ilefos tracks between atoms bind them together.

Atomic Phase Displacement
- An energy conversion in an atom. This takes place in neutrons and protons.

Atomic quark
- A type of quark that controls other quarks.

Atomic quarks
- See atomic quark.

Dielectricity
- The most common energy in the universe and dark energy's main energy component. It is created in matter, stars and black holes.

Dielectricity release
- When dielectricity detaches itself from ilefos tracks and becomes free dielectricity, a main component of dark energy.

Energy-nuclear quarks
- See energy quark

Energy quark
- An energy quark is a type of quark whose main task is to create and store energy, primarily dielectricity.

ER energy
- This is a type of energy that is primarily used for communication, but which can be converted. This is a dimension energy.

Photons

- O Photons, or light, are quarks emitted from matter to handle high levels of energy. Photons consist of between 3 and 7 quarks which are charged with energy. The light's wavelength is dependent on how much energy and how many quarks a photon contains. Photon is a dynamic particle that can absorb or emit energy. The quarks contained in photons can be absorbed by matter. Photons are created through a process whereby certain matter receives too much energy and rids itself of quarks and energy, thereby creating photons. Photons are lightly affected by ilefos.

Free dielectricity

- O Dielectricity that is not bound to the atomic nucleus but that is free energy. It is bound in smaller energy units and is a main component of dark energy. It becomes free dielectricity after dielectricity release has taken place.

Free ilefos

- O Free ilefos is ilefos/gravity that is not bound to an atomic nucleus. It is smaller units of ilefos that are not attached to the tracks of an atom. Free ilefos is formed after ilefos release has taken place, and is a component of dark energy. It can accumulate in ilefos bubbles/gravitational fields.

Gravitang

- O Gravitang is the different track angles of ilefos tracks. The angles are determined by the amount of ilefos power in an ilefos track.

Gravity 23

- O Gravity is another word for ilefos. Gravity is most powerful when ilefos is bound to the atomic nucleus or ilefos source. Gravity 23 is a name for the extra gravity in gases that have extra negative quark, for example in oxygen. Oxygen's extra power in ilefos tracks create strong bounding with matter, creating extra strong ilefos tracks or gravity.

Gravity/ilefos bubbles

- O Gravity or ilefos bubbles are accumulations of free ilefos that are not attached to atoms. They have weak gravity and collect in large gravitational fields or bubbles in the universe.

Gravitational field

- O See gravity bubbles.

Ilefos release

- O Ilefos release takes place when ilefos loses contact with the atomic nucleus and becomes free ilefos.

Isotopes

- Isotopes are elements with additional energy quarks or quarks of the type basic nuclear quark type 1 or 2. This gives the element special properties.

Basic nuclear quark type 1

- Nuclear quark type 1 is a quark that must exist in matter. It must be present in order for atoms to form bonds.

Basic nuclear quark type 2

- Nuclear quark type 2 is almost always necessary and is present in nearly all atoms.

Basic nuclear quarks

- Basic nuclear quarks are quarks of the type 1 and 2. They are necessary quarks in normal matter.
  Normal matter can manage without some nuclear quarks type 2, but this is uncommon.

Control quarks

- Nuclear quarks that control the atoms' functions, communication and Atomic Phase Displacement.

Quark Oler

- An accumulation of quarks needed for Atomic Phase Displacement. They control Atomic Phase Displacement and are found in the central and upper parts of the atomic nucleus, neutron and proton.

Quarks

- The building blocks of atomic nuclei, photons and resa. Quarks in atoms are divided into 4 main types: Basic nuclear quarks, special quarks, uni-quarks and control quarks.

  Basic nuclear quark type 1:

  1. Energy quark – A type of quark that primarily works with energies; storing, extracting and converting.
  2. Plus quark – A quark that is mainly involved in ilefos, primarily sending and receiving ilefos via ilefos tracks.
  3. Negative quark – A quark that works with internal communication in an atom.
  4. Omega quark – A quark that mainly works with omega energy, a dimension energy.
  5. ER quark – A quark that mainly works with ER energy and communication. A dimension energy.

Basic nuclear quark type 2:

6. TE quark – A quark that primarily works with TE energy.
7. Tre quark – A quark that primarily works with Tre energy and communication between atoms.
8. IS quark – A quark that is involved in IS energy.
9. IQ quark – A quark that is involved in an internal process in an atom.
10. Plus quark 2 – A quark that mainly works with ilefos and energies, in addition to Atomic Phase Displacement.
11. Neutral quark – A quark that primarily works with internal and external transport of information in an atom.
12. Tinga quark – A quark that primarily works with Atomic Phase Displacement.
13. Alpha quark (α quark) – a quark that primarily works with alpha energy.
14. Omega 2 quark – A quark that primarily works with storing and converting omega energy.
15. In quark – A quark that primarily works with incoming communication to an atom.
16. Out quark – A quark that primarily works with outgoing communication from an atom.
17. Plus quark 3 – A quark that primarily works with energies and ilefos.
18. Yr 2 quark – A quark that primarily works with storing and converting Yr energy.
19. Yr 1 quark – A quark that primarily works with sending and receiving Yr energy.
20. Yt 1 quark – A quark that primarily works with sending and receiving Yt energy.
21. Yt 2 quark – A quark that primarily works with storing and converting Yt energy.
22. TE quark 2 – A quark that primarily works with storing and converting TE energy.
23. Plus quark 3 – A quark that primarily works with energies and ilefos.

Matter

Ọ A system of atoms with nuclei, uniparticl-es and gravity/ilefos. Normal matter has 256 quarks (256-290). Matter mainly consists of resa, normal matter and dark matter.

Dark energy

Ọ Energy that is not bound to matter, stars or black holes. Dark energy makes up about 70% of the universe. It is composed of:

Free dielectricity	65%
Free ilefos	15%
Omega	15%
Other energies	5%

Dark matter

O Matter that has been exposed to huge amounts of energy and has created extra quarks to handle this extra amount. Dark matter has particularly powerful ilefos and energy tracks and absorbs photons and energy. It does not generally reflect photons/light and has between 290 and 350 quarks. Dark matter is found at the centre of planets, stars and most celestial bodies.

Negative quark

O A quark that mainly works with communication.

Omega energy

O A form of energy emitted by matter, stars and black holes. This is described in more detail in the second book, 'Bent theory of the universe, energies, gravity and atoms'. This is a dimension energy.

Omega quark

O Omega quarks work with Omega energy contained in matter.

Plus quark

O Plus quarks work with ilefos in the atom.

Radioactive elements

O Elements with additional energy quarks and that have particularly high amounts of energy stored in them.

Resa

O A simple form of matter containing 8–255 quarks that do not have ilefos tracks.

Resa 0

O Resa 0 is simple quark compositions without uniparticles that have 8–50 quarks without uniparticles or ilefos tracks.

Special quarks

O A type of quark that is not of a standard type. They can vary a great deal and are not essential to matter/atoms.

TE energy

O A form of energy

Tre energy

O A form of energy

Tre quark

O A quark that works with Tre energy.

Uni-quarks

- A special quark that must exist in atoms, which is involved in neutrons, protons and uniparticles. Uni-quarks ensure internal communication in the atomic nucleus. They can be in several different places simultaneously.

Uniparticles

- Uniparticles are particles orbiting the atomic nucleus. Uniparticles stabilise ilefos tracks and atoms. They have weak gravity and have a repulsive force on other uniparticles. Uniparticles are an important component of atoms.

WE energy

- A form of energy.

Yr energy

- A form of energy.

AUTHOR

Figure 31: Author Bent Rolf Pettersen

Bent Rolf Pettersen was born in Bergen, Norway, in 1967. He has a business education and has founded and managed several companies, developed a number of technologies and submitted a number of patents.

He has a great interest in physics and astronomy. This resulted in years of research in the field and the development of new theories in the area of physics and astronomy.

This book, 'Bent theory of atoms, energies and gravity', attempts to explain these theories.

The next book will delve deeper into the theories and provide mathematical explanations for them.